Queen of Penny Pinching
by Kate Singh

D1744573

Queen of Penny Pinching
Living a Royal, Spiritual and Joyful Life on Pennies

By Kate Singh

website: www.mrskatesingh.com
blog: www.katesinghsite.wordpress.com
email: vondola@yahoo.com

Table of Contents

Introduction....The Queen

Chapter 1....The Beginning of Your New Life

Chapter 2....Downsizing the Castles and other Royal Expenses

Chapter 3....Declutter and Scrubbing the Castle

Chapter 4....Bill Trimming Time

Chapter 5....Trim the Fat Off the Grocery Bill

Chapter 6....Downsizing the Royal Garage

Chapter 7....Making an Inexpensive Royal Baby

Chapter 8....Royal Beauty

Chapter 9....Having Fun is Priceless

Chapter 10....Decorating the Castle

Chapter 11....Staying Home

Chapter 12....Royal Holidays

Chapter 13....A Spiritual Practice is Free

Chapter 14....Paying Off the Royal Debt

Chapter 15....Tips and Secrets of the Wise

References

Introduction

The Queen's Story

My story is like many out there. A young girl with student loans to a college that I never complete, my first car loan on a not so great car and then being offered credit everywhere I went…and taking it gleefully.

Within less than a couple of years I was in debt up to my ears and not so gleeful. I pulled out my basket of integrity and worked hard for almost 8 years to pay every penny back. This meant 2 jobs normally and 3 during holidays. You know the Beatles song 8 days a week? That was my week. I worked and toiled my youth away. I also lived meagerly, not being able to choose what castle I lived in or what work I did or how much work I had to do. As much as I worked I never had money. One part of this dilemma was paying the large debt and the other problem was that I wasn't good with budgeting. I always loved the idea of penny pinching, however I wasn't practicing the art.

When my mother passed away she left me a mini fortune. I used it wisely to pay off the last of my debt and to purchase, in full, a used car (this time a quality car that would last to infinity).

I even paid off her remaining debt (in runs in the family). I was free! Wow, how great that felt to not lie awake at 3 am to wonder how to pay all the bills or to have to live in a rented room in someone else's castle or a tiny, ugly studio, because it's all I could afford with all the burden of my debts and car payments. I had freedom to not work for a while, to rest after 8 years of work, work and work on top of work.

I could choose the job carefully, I could choose what kind of dwelling I wanted to nest in, I could eat out, go to the movies, shop and shop and shop. And there began the next lesson.

It was wonderful after years of debt and work confinement to spend money freely, but I blew through my little royal fortune quickly because I hadn't learned the 2nd lesson of budgeting and frugality and I wound up with nothing to show for that inheritance. However, I didn't and haven't ever gotten into debt again; never had another credit card and I purchase everything with cash, even my cars.

I began to really learn the art of frugality and being wonderfully cheap in the last few years after I married a man who is very good with money and can save like a champion. We live off one income and I enjoy being a stay at home mother to my two boys.

We've had some life changes that created money challenges. One of those challenges came when my spouse was out of a job due to a business going under. We had to move, take a job that was not so great and the income was half of what we were used to. I really had to learn the art of frugality and making the penny stretch. That is when I started studying like crazy. I read tons of books from the library, internet articles, blogs and

YouTube videos made from families living on tight budgets. I have compiled a list of books and websites to help you in the back of this book, however I suggest you do your own research. There are so many housewives that blog and YouTube about how they budget, shop, clean, save and got out of debt. Whatever you need help with you will find on the wonderful internet.

This book is a collection of all that I have learned. It won't help you with investments and it won't teach you to be a Martha Stewart, but it will help you if you want to get out of debt, save tons of dough, live off one income or just work part time and pursue other endeavors.

This book also encourages everyone to be conscious shoppers and to make a difference on this planet both environmentally and with humanity and to think about the future for our children. We can make powerful changes individually by what we do at home with our families. How, where and what we shop for and what business's we support. We want a better planet and we can make that happen. We as the consumers actually control the companies. They only change when forced by the consumer's trend. It is the corporations that we really need to change to make huge impacts on the environment and humanity right?

I have fallen to the thrill of a dollar coffee at McDonalds, however I try to shop locally and support my Co-ops and local organic farms. We need to recycle, reuse and compost, not waste and growing your own food. Let's not support companies that are polluters or are causing destruction with their practices and mistreatments of their workers. Try walking whenever possible or supporting public transportation, that way we are being part of the solution and becoming consciences consumers. That creates a peace of mind and a wholesome life.

There are 3 levels to this book, beginner, intermediate and hard core. You choose what works for you and take what you like and leave the rest...or go hard core and make huge changes in your lives. Either way, make it fun and enjoy the process. Make it into a game and you will begin to see the benefits. It's exciting starting a new life style with positive goals, but it can quickly become mundane. My suggestion is to find stories like yours, find people that are living this frugal way and can keep you inspired. Every once in a while you may need to splurge or ease up and readjust things to fit you and your family. Play with it.

Let's get started!!!

Chapter 1

The Beginning of Your New Life

So, I'm not a banker or financial expert, however I do have some great advice on taking charge of the finances and getting out of debt. I have learned by my own field work and listening to the wise elders. In under taking this big life change please take what you like and can do comfortably. You can tweak and adjust as time goes by and you can move up to more advanced steps as you get used to all this change.

I'm going to start with the big stuff that gets us in trouble. I'm orchestrating this manual as though you are in debt or just need a major over haul. When doing a major over haul you have to look at your life and home from the inside out.

Let's begin with the big stuff and then we will make it all the way down to the cleaning out of closets and taking a look at the grocery budget.

First thing to do when in financial doo doo is to sit down for a long session of research and discovery. If you have more going out then the paycheck can cover, we need to fix that first. We need to start cutting back and gaining control and then we can think about what to do with the debt. You need money to tackle debt, so we need to find out where all that money is going and see if we can free some of it up.

Find a place in your home that is comfortable such as the kitchen table or your desk and make sure you have some uninterrupted time to really focus and think. This is a big life changing moment right now.

You will need:

pen
pencil
paper
highlighters in various colors
laptop (optional)
bank statements or access to a printer
bills
calculator
pot of coffee
aspirin

Start by making a list of all your expenses. That would be all your monthly bills and priorities like mortgage/rent, electricity, garbage, water and so on. Next add to the list all the extras such as entertainment, latte's, dinners out, etc.

Get out a month or two of bank statements or print them up off line. You are going to highlight everything in sections. It's wise to look at least two to three months or more of spending to really get an idea of what's happening with your finances. Now choose a color for the priorities such as your rent/mortgage, electric, cell phone, water, garbage and whatever else you feel is a need.

You will choose a separate color for all groceries and another color for entertainment, another color for clothes and so on. You group things and color them however you like.

Now you get to really see where all that money is going and if you have never done this and it's been unchecked...WHOO

WHEE!! This is where the aspirin comes in. No, don't start drinking, you still have a lot of homework.

Now for the fun part! Now you go through the bank statements and, on a separate piece of paper, you will start out make columns with titles such as "fun shopping", coffees, entertainment, and meals out. Another section is devoted to groceries and another to gas. Make as many sections as you need or however you want to divide it up. Then you total up all that you have spent in each section. You must be really honest and detailed. When you total up groceries you add up every single, dingle time you have gone to the store, even that midnight quart of ice cream.

You should probably take a break and eat something, hydrate a bit before this next section. No, still not time to start drinking.

Alright my Viking! Now the big bills list. This is where you may need to scan the bank statements or bills and see what you pay for electricity, garbage and such. Rent or mortgage stays the same, but gas and electric can fluctuate so guestimate for the seasons. My bill for gas is lowest in summer and sky high in winter.

When you are done with all the sections, add them up. You should have a total of your spending for each category for each month.

Ok, you are done. Now you can have a drink and take the evening off. You might need the evening to process all you have learned about yourself. Sleep on it. We will get started on the cleanup in the next few chapters.

And remember, I'm not a financial analyst, I have no degree in real estate and I have no clue how to rock the investment world. I'm a simple lady with solid advice. I've been in your shoes and I now live a great life on the other side, after years of mistakes and victories. I have lived it, done it, did it, fixed it, researched it, and made it to the other side. You will have to make the big and hard decisions for your personality and what lifestyle you really want. Like I said in the Queen's Story, you can do 3 different levels: beginners, half way or hard core. It all depends on what you want to accomplish and how fast. It also can be traumatic to rush into such great changes...or it can be super fun! Play with it.

See you in the next pages for some fun work ahead!

Chapter 2

Downsizing the Castle and Other Royal Expenses

Mortgage out of control? Rent to high? Depending on where you live this may take some magic. Your blood pressure may be rising as you start to read this, but there is hope...always!

Owning

If you own your castle and your biggest headache is the mortgage, ask yourself if it's all worth it? Visualize yourself 5 years from now, 10 years, 15, 25...can you keep up the mortgage nightmare for that long? What if you lose a job, if you have a partner/spouse, what if they lose a job? What if one of you gets sick, injured, put on disability? I know, I love this kind of talk too. Really lifts one's spirits. But it's serious stuff. We can't be weak now. It's time to get real and ask the hard questions. Are you prepared for an emergency or life change?

So let's look at your castle and if it's affordable. If you have a mortgage, can you refinance? Double payments and get it paid off quickly? Would you be willing to get a second job to make bigger payments or maybe you need an extra job just to pay the normal payment (that would be sad and unsustainable long term)? How about rent it out and move to a tiny and cheap hut and get a second job and get the mortgage done. So, the big question here is, what would it take to pay off your mortgage as fast as possible. Or maybe you are just trying to not drown and you are looking at decades of these big payments.

 Here are other ideas: get a roommate or two (however many rooms you have). Some roommates are wonderful and provide companionship and community, ever watch The Golden Girls? We will discuss this later (not the Golden Girls, but roommates).

When making decisions big and small use this technique: picture yourself doing it, living it, going to it, whatever "it" may be and see how it feels. For example, if you wanted to move to another town, picture doing the move and living in the house, walking in the neighborhood, shopping at the local mart. How did you feel? Now, picture you not doing the move, staying where you are and doing all the same stuff. How does that feel? Did you feel joy, relief, excitement or stagnant. Fear is a feeling that comes with all new and unknown things, but there are always other powerful emotions that are more reliable than fear. Fear is false emotion appear real. I learned that off a news letter.

How does it "feel" to think about letting the house go? If it feels like a great relief think about selling or maybe you're in too deep and need to just file bankruptcy. You are one of many these days. House sales and rentals are out of control in some areas, but you don't need to be a part of it. You *can* walk away if it's a sinking ship of debt. It's the ego that hangs on.

Renting

Now, if you are renting it's a bit easier to change this situation if it's a big pain. Once again, you can get a roommate. Roommates are fun to have coffee with and chat about our latest date (maybe your spouse is your roommate so forget that). If that won't work, is the lease almost up? Start looking for something more affordable. Try new neighborhoods where rent is easier on the wallet. Don't be afraid of the "other side". We live in a working class neighbor hood with some rough parts and fabulous parts. We have some not so attractive areas down the way. But sometimes you take the good with the not so good and it turned out to be the best move we've made and we are very happy and safe.

So, think outside the box, look outside your area, town, even state. Why people spend more on rent and mortgages I don't get. It used to be recommended, in the old days, that you spend only 1/4th of your monthly income…maybe it was 1/3rd. Either way, people are now spending half their income, if they are lucky; some are spending 3/4ths. That is madness. You have no quality of life. You are just living and struggling to have a roof over your head, but you're never under your roof because you are out working your royal tushy off.

So, is that 5 bedroom worth it? Or that rental in the prime part of the city? I think not. Think of how you would live if your rent or mortgage was half what it is. How are you going to do that?

Here's the action plan. I'm about seeing the problem, crying for a few minutes, go through the emotions and then find a solution, fix it and move on to the fun times. If you aren't, then give this book to someone else and get a book about working through emotions at a snail's pace.

Solutions for a renter or owner

 If you are a home owner, decide if you can refinance, get a roommate or two, rent out the whole house, sell (even if it's a short sale) or foreclose. You may want to get the professionals involved, however once you know what you want to do *don't* let anyone talk you out of it and keep you stuck. If you are in over your head throw in the towel for God's sake!

If you rent, get a roommate, ask your landlord/lady to reduce the rent. This depends on what kind of relationship you have, how long you've been there and if there has been an economic down turn since you moved in and sometimes a landlord will reduce the rent in hard times to keep good tenants. If none of this really works, find out when your lease is up and start looking elsewhere.

Start looking at affordable rents and then take some Sunday drives through those neighborhoods, both in the morning and evening to see what it feels like. For example, I look for lots of family activity in a neighborhood such as children playing outside, people out taking walks, and grandmas outside pruning their roses. I steer away from the neighborhoods with lots of scruffy people just hanging around and quiet, lifeless streets. All depends on what you want to live in.

When choosing another abode for yourself and maybe a family or perhaps just your dog or cat, you must make a list. What are your must haves and what can you live without (even if you have a major mood swing around possibly having to go without). If you have children and/or pets, they have needs such as a backyard, playgrounds or what not. Really whittle that list down. I know we are in the New Age of dreaming and believing that "You can have it all!", but that may have been the thinking that got you into this situation. It's time to be realistic.

When going for size, go small. The smaller the house the less the energy bills, the less time to clean, the easier to maintain and it's amazing what one can do with a tiny yard. You can work with anything when you have the right attitude. In most European and Asian countries whole families live in tiny houses.

Where do you think IKEA came about? It started out making furniture to accommodate and utilize small spaces; because in Sweden most of the homes are small (I may have over heard this or made some of it up). Only in America do we go big with our big house, big car, big, big and big. But guess what? We are realizing, as a culture, that big is a pain in the arse. The new movement is tiny. Tiny houses are very popular now and cars are getting smaller too, look at the compact SUV.

I have a husband, two little boys, two average sized dogs and a cat. We downsized from a 2,000 square foot house with 2 living rooms, 3 bedrooms, 2 bathrooms (kinda wish we still had the two bathrooms) and a huge yard in the front and back. We downsized to an 860 square foot, 2 bedrooms, 1 bath house with one little yard. We are very happy in our cozy, tiny castle. It takes 30 minutes to clean the whole house (maybe more if I'm really cleaning), our utilities are way down, rent is much less and we have a much better quality of life because I can play with the boys, write, read and just have fun instead of cleaning and doing yard work all day to maintain the place.

So, only have what you need and no more. Go from the ritzy downtown to maybe the working class neighborhood or the artsy alcoves. Get rid of the big house and get a one or two bedroom. You don't need 5 bedrooms, do you? If you're worried about future guest, buy a pull out couch. Ditch the 3 acres of lawn for a little backyard garden (also very hip these days).

Alright, that should be enough to chew on for this session. See you in the next chapter. We will be talking about downsizing all that is now in the house or takes to run a house. This will be especially handy if you plan to move and move into something smaller.

Adios for now!

Chapter 3

Decluttering and Scrubbing the Castle

Well now, we have tackled some huge stuff right? By now you have the big picture on your finances, such as how much is going out and where it's all going. We've discussed the rent or mortgage and if that's sustainable. What we are going to do now is stop talking finances and money for a little bit, take a break from such heavy topics and start doing some spring cleaning! Yay! Don't fret we will get right back to the bills and fixing your finances in the next chapters.

Right now I want to focus on the state of your home. I personally find it is really important to get the castle in order so that you can think. I also find that cleaning is like therapy and I figure out some of my biggest dilemmas as I organize my home. Once my house is clean and spacious, I feel like I can breathe and I get motivated to tackle all sorts of other task. It's the physical act of cleaning up and clearing out that is very healing and proactive, leading to more proactive behavior. Cleaning and de cluttering is energy work and it brings balance and order to chaos. This is truly the beginning of your journey. Let's get crackin' on the clutter!

Let's start by setting a date for a garage sale. This way you have a deadline to get things done and you can also be motivated by the idea of making some cash. Give yourself a week only. I find that under pressure we will move fast and not hem and haw too much and decide that we really need to save that old shirt and keep this ratty piece of furniture. Move fast, less thought, more doing. Have a friend help, someone hard core. You need a whip cracking friend right now, not someone to hold your hand.

You can also sell items online. It's a great way to make money. Take pictures of items and post. If an item won't sell, then take it to the thrift store. In my neighborhood I can put stuff on the curb with a free sign and it's gone by the end of the day. Just don't put out junky stuff, then you're just trashing your neighborhood.

Go from room to room with bags and boxes. Make piles, one is trash, one is for the garage sale or thrift store. There may even be some items you give to friends and family. People love freebies. One man's trash is another's treasure right?

Get rid of all the chachka that just collects dust, clothes you haven't worn in years or since you were 15 pounds lighter, get rid of extra furniture that just takes up space, but isn't used or sat on. Anything stained, ripped, broken, shabby. Get rid of items that were given to you and you're not really into, but keep to be kind. Get rid of anything that has a funky vibe. Sometimes we keep photos and other things that are less than complimentary or that make us feel less than happy when we look at them. Out they go! Only keep what you really love and use. Give stuff away; give to neighbors, the thrift store, and the man on the street. Practice the art of giving.

Go through every room and work from the outside in. Once you have cleared the outside space, go into the closets and drawers. You will need a garbage bag for the drawers, because drawers are where we throw every piece of junk we want to clear off the counter. Get rid of it, that collection of bottle caps, old tooth picks, business cards we never used, that thingamajig and pieces of furniture we never re attached. Ah, that feels so good, now wipe the drawer clean and put back the good stuff you use.

Into the closets we go! Get rid of anything you haven't worn in a very long time, that you never wear, but say you will, anything ripped, torn (unless you really do love it and wear it and will mend it, then put it in a fix it pile), stained beyond repair, too small, too big, ugly, not flattering, given by someone else and not your taste. Thrift stores here we come! Don't forget to go through your shoes too.

Now let's look at the state of your linens and towels and such. All the torn, holy (and I don't mean saint) towels and blankets can go to the animal shelters, they need stuff like this. Stained and dingy dish towels and sheets that have lost the elastic and have stains and holes, you can do a couple things, one is get rid of them and two is to rip them up and turn them into cleaning rags.

Time to hit the bathroom. Let's get rid of all the old medications (make sure to dispose of them properly, check with your local pharmacist if not sure), lotions, outdate sunscreens, old packets of dental floss that may cause gingivitis if used, old make up (especially mascara). Donate any products that may be still fine, but you don't use. Downsize to only the stuff you use and meds you use once in a while such as baby Tylenol for the little person. Splurge and get new tooth brushes for the whole family. You may have perfumes or scented lotions and make up in good shape that you could gift to a friend?

How are you feeling? You should be feeling good about now and like you have room to breathe, unless you are a pack rat and then you probably aren't doing this at all and should give this book away and get a book on how to build more shelves and storage.

Ok, now the garage. Oh, I know, the garage sucks. Not as fun as inside. Get going. Go fast. Keep all the tools and yard stuff and car repair stuff. Get rid of all the junk you have been saving for "someday". Neighbors, especially guys, love stuff from the garage. Got to clean it out to prepare for the garage sale! Now garages are tricky because there is stuff in there you may only use once in a blue moon, but you don't want to get rid of it so don't. You want to just get all the extra junk out and you know in your heart what that is. If you are moving to somewhere without a garage or a smaller one, take that into consideration and move it out. Once you are done, give it a good sweeping and smile at all the work you have accomplished.

Don't forget the backyard; there is always a broken piece of lawn chair or deflated ball that can't be revived. Clean it out sister (or brother)!

Now, go have a drink or piece of cake and celebrate! I highly encourage celebrating after each task. You are doing amazing life changing things right now. It is Metaphysical Law that the more you clear out space, be it physical or emotional; you make room for new things to come in. Also, all things, people and places hold and have energy...a vibration. When you clean and clear out space physically, you are also doing it on a mental, emotional level leading to a change in your vibration.

When you start to make changes, no matter how small, you send a message to the Universe that you are ready for something new, something that serves you and/or your family better. You will receive it, always know that as you move forward you will be supported and served well by the Universe surrounding you. Watch, it will show up in tiny ways, then small moments, then a big blessing here and a miracle there. Be grateful for all of it, every drop, say thank you and embrace the moment. Each moment of gratitude expands into more blessings. Each time you give to others, with time or stuff, you get back, each time you clean up a space, you raise the vibration.

That is why it is so important to get rid of all that does not serve you or has a negative feel to it. Even a chair in the living room that you feel irritated with each time you look at it...remove it.

This process should be very deep and thorough. Sometimes you may need to just set something aside for a day or so before you can let it go. Give yourself some time, but not too much. You know what you really need or use or love the first time.

Good luck!

Chapter 4

Bill Trimming Time

Time to save some money!!! Are you excited? You should be. Do this early in the morning or late at night if you are a night owl. Pick a time when you work well, get a pot of coffee brewing or something refreshing to stay hydrated. Get out the pen and paper, calculator, laptop, bills and statements again. We are going back to the desk for some number crunching.

Ok, now listen, you have to be super willing and get hard core again. Of course you don't *have* to do anything, but then you should just give this book away and get a book on how to live over your limit and constantly stress and struggle.

We already started with the house situation. That's done. Now let's look at our monthly bills:
Cell
House phone
Gas
Electric
Garbage
Water
Cable/dish
Internet
Car insurance
Health insurance
House insurance
Life Insurance

You may have other things here that I'm missing. We are just looking at utilities and house bills right now. If you have more than these basics, like yard maintenance, house cleaning service, a cook...decide if you really need it and if you can do it yourself or have the service maybe once a month rather than every week.

Home and cell phones are great, but do you need a home and cell? Can you do with just one phone? Choose which one. I chose home over cell. I love being away from the phone when I leave the house. I don't worry about losing my phone, dropping and breaking my phone or not having clear reception. Whatever works best for you either cell or home phone. Now whittle your plan down as much as you can. Can you do with just a basic plan? Or are you doing business and need the full plan? Can you find a cheaper carrier? There is so much competition out there that you can find great deals for the cell phone. There are great plans for the home phone also, you just have to investigate. Get plans that are just one flat rate a month so you don't have to figure out your bill every month. Take the headache out of it. Don't be afraid to have a bare bones plane if you really need to cut cost and don't really have to have all the bells and whistles.
Your friends and family will still love you.

Internet and cable. Get the super cheap internet. You don't need the speed of light.... or, get rid of it! Go to the library.

Cable or Dish, you don't need it, especially all the movie channels. I've had them and they show the same darn movies today that they were showing 5 years ago. You can get all kinds of movies and shows online (if you keep your internet), or the $1.00 movie rental boxes. You can also get an antenna. You will get all the local channels for free. That's all you need. There, just saved you $100 plus. If you got rid of internet too, maybe you have save $200 or more. If you keep internet you can get Netflix streaming for $7.99 or Hulu or whatever else is out there now for movies and TV series and it's a fraction of the cost of Dish or Cable. If you get rid of internet, you can order tons of movies through the library.

Insurance is tricky. If you rent and don't have to have it, drop it. On the other hand, it is usually cheap. Just look into what it really covers and what kind of damage as far as fires and floods. Health insurance is a must have, many persons have gone into debt with medical emergencies. Especially if you have kids. Car insurance is a must have, but maybe you can find a better and less expensive company. If you don't drive much cut it down to partial and cut your bill in half. Talk to your agent. Life insurance is great if married with or without kids. This is a safety net if something happens to you spouse. Make sure everyone is covered in all emergencies or in the unfortunate case of death. Also, a good life insurance will help you if your spouse gets sick and can't work. Know your insurances.

Gas and electric, water and garbage. I think garbage is a flat rate. However, gas and electric can be reduced greatly with proper and conservative use.

Ways to save on energy cost:
Summer

- Lots of advice givers suggest setting the thermostat for summer and winter. I don't know how much that saves. I just use it when I need it.
- In the summer I only use the AC when it's in the triple digits and I don't turn it on until after noon and I shut is off by 5 or 6 in the evening.
- Use lots of open windows and fans and to feel great. When in summer it's best to leave windows open all night and morning, run a whole house fan if you have it. As soon as it's getting warm shut everything up. As soon as it starts cooling down open everything up. Work with nature.
- Go green and plant lots of trees around your house. You can save up to 40% on utilities when the trees get big and provide shade and protections.

Winter

- In winter get thick curtains to keep heat in if you have single pane windows. Or get them anyway.
- Huge area rugs keep heat from seeping through floors.
- Get out the thick comforters and flannel sheets.
- Wear sweaters, get a great pair of slippers and keep the heat low.
- If you have a wood stove, you can try and find wood cheap or free.
- If it's your home, think about investing in double pane windows, it makes a huge difference.
- Think about going solar. Some cities are offering to install for free through some programs linked with local energy companies.

- PG and E offers an energy saver program, if you are low income, where they will come in and do some upkeep and repairs to make your house more energy efficient. They may even replace your frig or dryer. Check it out. It's surprising how much help is out there.
- Keep lights off all the time, except what you need. Unplug unused items. Take advantage of candle light and white Christmas lights. The combination can be very charming.

Water, you know the drill.
- Short showers, don't run water while brushing teeth, don't wash drive way, do the car wash at the gas station.
- You can put buckets under faucets and shower heads to catch water while you wait for it to heat up. You save gallons that way and can then use that extra water on house plants and your garden.
- Water garden carefully, don't have broken or lame sprinklers. Switch out a lawn for a garden.
- Use mulch to conserve water. Mulch retains 70% more water on gardens, trees and plants (I read that on a T-shirt at a gardening center). Your local water company will give you tons of ideas on how to save water.

Those are the main bills. Start trimmin'.

Chapter 5

Trim the Fat Off the Grocery Bill

Let's get out those bank statements that had all the trips to the grocery store hi lighted. Add up a month or two. What did you get? Was it a shock? Now, let's look at all the meals out, lunches out of the office, dinners out all week, even if just weekends, all the coffees and cappuccino's, the trips to the corner store for a snack, the bakery with the divine muffins. How much money are you spending a week, a month, even in a day?

Let's get started! First we STOP everything. All the extra trips to the store, all the eating out, coffees out, no more bakery, take a break from the corner mart. This won't be forever, we just need to clear the board and buckle down to get the spending under control. Later we can start going out again, but in a new and frugal way.

Now we go major grocery shopping! We are going to recreate all your café and dining out experiences from home. We will need lots of coffee beans and the fixin's (creamer, sugar, whatever you put in your coffee cocktail), snacks, things to pack in lunches, breakfast foods, and dinner items.

But before you go shopping let's clean out the frig and cupboards and assess what you already have and can use. You need to sit down with paper and pen and think about this. What do you want for a week's worth of breakfast, what will pack well for lunch, what do you and the family like for dinners? Snacking and coffee are super important at my house. I love to bake and we have to have popcorn for movies. The goal here is to stock your kitchen so you don't need to go out. You should have everything there. You want to start practicing cooking everything at home, packing meals and snacks from home, having your own coffee house...at home! Make it fun; even get yourself one of those espresso machines if you have to, life is short, make this whole frugal, new budget, new life thing a game!

Now that you have cleaned out the kitchen and stocked it up, now what? Menu time! Menu planning is easy. You write out a 7 day week. 7 breakfast, 7 lunches, 7 dinners. Do it in rows or charts, print something off the internet, whatever works for you. Think about what you and the family like for breakfast, what is easy and packable for lunches, and yummy, healthy dinners. Get ideas off the internet. There are lots of websites where housewives will give ideas on menu planning and meal ideas. Pinterest is great for quick ideas for lunches to pack for kids and worker bees. You can also start looking up budget ideas for dinners. Aaah, I love the internet, you can get a whole PhD on budgeting and cooking.

Envelope Please

- Now, from here on out we do an envelope budget system. This will make all the difference in your new world.

- You have 4 envelopes, one envelope for each week.

- You allow yourself so much cash for each week of groceries. You do not go over; you only use what you have. This is where meal planning for the week comes in handy.

- You make your menu and then you make a grocery list of what you need to make that menu plan happen.

- You then plan one day a week to do the shopping. Pick a day and time that you can go slowly and try a few stores. Eventually, you will know which stores you save the most and you'll have your favorites.

- Take a calculator and your shopping list and any coupons you may have. Look at prices at each store until you find the best prices.

As for finding the best priced stores, you can ask your neighbors, get online information, ask the locals. There are also Farmers Markets that are great for fresh, local produce and supports the local farmers and being sustainable. Anytime you can go Green, support local businesses and be GMO free and organic...do it! Being organic is getting more affordable as it gets more popular and I am willing to spend more on clean, GMO free food and less on medical bills in the future. Your local health food stores have weekly and monthly deals and you can save by joining as an owner and buying in bulk.

We all have a comfort level and things we just can't do without. Do not create suffering or lack. This will make you throw this book away and gorge on cake. All this frugal and new budgeting stuff can be tailored to fit any personality. Some will go so hard core it will make a penny cry. Some of you will still have to budget in the daily trip to the coffee house, because that's your happy place. Please, find your happy place.

I can budget like a pro, but I won't compromise my family's health. I am very pro sustainable, local and organic, regenerative farming. I spend some extra bucks on good, quality food. Where I cut corners would be at the salon, going out to eat, the lattes out. I cut out enough extras that it more than makes up for the money I spend at the local Co-op (my happy place). I also, do a majority of shopping discount stores. In some areas you can find employee owned grocery outlets and they tend to have better prices.

So, you have the menu plan, the grocery list, the calculator, your favorite stores and your shopping day, now what? Now we decide how much to spend.

Start by totaling up all you used to spend on groceries and going out and cut it in half. If you spent $800 on groceries and $500 on all the meals, lunches and coffees that you purchased outside the home, that is a shocking $1300. This is more an estimate for a family and very easy to spend in this day and in my California state. So, half would be $650. You aren't going out anymore (or for now) and that is plenty for groceries. Divide that into 4 envelopes.

Start there and as you master the stores, the price comparisons, and a few more tricks I'm about to share, you can see how much you can trim each week. Make sure it's comfortable, but make it into a game.

Tips for the hardcore shopper

Now for some more advanced tricks since you have the basics down.

- Cut out all the sodas, beer, wine, booze. Coffee is your luxury item and water is so good for you. Juice is sugar and extra calories, soda is horrible for you (anything that deteriorates pipes can't be easy on the bladder) and booze, beer, wine, that just ads to the waistline. If you must have it, try to cut way back.

- Milk isn't really necessary either, you can get plenty of calcium from greens and other sources.

- Do popcorn as a snack and ditch all the cookies and junk. Sugar is the devil! Take this new budget opportunity to also clean up eating habits and get super healthy. You can put butter, nutritional yeast, cheese powder, basil, all kinds of fun stuff to make yummy popcorn snacks. You can even make kettle corn or caramel corn. Popcorn is versatile and cheap (make sure it's non GMO).

- Fruit and nuts are great snacks, along with carrots and celery dipped in ranch...YUMMMMMM EEE!

- All wise and health conscious shoppers will advise you that the biggest rule when shopping is to stay around the outer edges of the market. This is where the produce, dairy and meat hang out (the real food). Don't venture into the middle isles (that is the junk food and fake food).

- Buy produce in season, you will save a fortune.

- Stick with main staples such as meat, fruit, veggies, rice, pasta and dairy.

- Find the daily sales; also find out if the store has a weekly sale/discount day.

- Buy day old breads or day old meats (just as good).

- Frozen and canned veggies are just as good for you.

- Find the deals on canned items. When you find a great deal on canned, frozen or dried goods that can be stored, go ahead and stock up.

- Buy in bulk when you can and see if the store will discount large bulk buys.

***Don't* buy anything that is packaged, pre made, precooked or processed. The four P's. This shoots the grocery bill way up.** We also don't eat these foods because they are loaded with chemicals, sugars, preservatives and all kinds of junk that is not good for us, especially our children's little bodies. I truly believe that all these childhood issues such as ADD, ADHD and so on are caused all by the junk and sugar we consume. You will see a huge improvement in your children once you clean up the diet.

When cooking, think like Asian countries. The bulk of their meals are rice and vegetables. They use very little meat or tofu. Just a little meat in a big pot of pasta or rice and lots of vegetables goes a long, long way. Even think about having a few meatless days a week, start with one and as you get more creative, add a day or two more. This will make a huge dent in your grocery bill.

The foundation foods are potatoes (sweet potatoes are the best, loaded with vitamins), brown rice, pastas and beans. Make these the bulk of your meal. I then fill up with vegetables, then a little meat or meat substitutes (when we are on our vegetarian kick). I usually cook breakfast and then one big lunch that we also eat later for dinner and I pack for my husband's lunch and dinner. I like to make a lot of casseroles, pot roast, crock pot food in the winter, soups and baked breads. I learned this trick from my mother, we always had a big pot of something simmering on the stove and would just eat on that through the day. This is great to do on weekends.

Lunches: if work has a microwave you can bring home cooked meals that need heating. If not, good ol' sandwiches, healthy chips, fruit, veggies, nuts and dried fruit are great. Pack big bags of popcorn to snack on if you tend to snack at work a lot. It'll curb the trip to the snack shack down the way. Pack your own water. A great hint: freeze waters the night before so it's ice cold for you or kids at school.

Coupons can be handy, but I really don't buy any of the stuff being couponed. Coupons are for the new products a company wants you to try and we don't buy junk food or fabric softeners. If you get a Sunday paper, go through it and save the coupons on oil changes, dry cleaning or a restaurant for the special treat. Sometimes it's fun to splurge on a burger and you can get a two for one. These are when coupons come in handy.

Toiletries and cleaning items.

- Buy tissue and detergents in bulk.

- If you feel really inspired, make your own laundry detergent and cleaners. They are very Green and very easy to make and will save you a lot of money and cupboard space. All you need for house cleaners is white vinegar, dish soap, rubbing alcohol, borax, and baking soda (lemons come in handy too).

- Baking soda can be used as scouring powder. Make into a paste and let sit 20 minutes for hard to clean areas.

When mixed with vinegar it can unclog drains. A lemon dipped in borax can clean sinks and such.

- Mix water, rubbing alcohol and vinegar for window cleaner.

- Mix water, vinegar and borax for cleaning floors and counters.

- For laundry detergent you'll need borax, washing soap and a bar of Ivory soap or Fels Naptha. You grate soap and mix one cup soap, ½ cup borax, ½ cup washing soap. Use TBSP for large loads of laundry.

There are lots of great sights online for making all kinds of homemade cleaners for everything you can imagine. Look it up for the proper recipes and ideas. Making your own cleaners is very inexpensive, but the biggest reason to be motivated to do this is that they are nontoxic to children and pets, they are environmentally friendly and don't put poisons in our homes, the earth, our waters and our air.

Paper towels. This is a luxury, as are paper napkins. I use cloth towels in the kitchen, cloth napkins, old towels and t-shirts for cleaning. I do have a stash of paper towels and they are only used to clean up the most hideous of messes such as poop, pee, puke, the three P's. I have two little boys, two dogs and a cat that leaves hair balls as gifts, a roll of paper towels is part of my emergency clean up kit.   You save a lot of pennies and trees when you stop buying these two products for everyday use.

Shampoos, conditioners, soap and other toiletries, I go to the discount stores and outlets and stock up on big deals. I have even found great make up there and buy a few extras. There are some frugal ways also.

- Buy toilette tissue in bulk.

- Coconut butter is great in place of lotions for body and face and babies. No chemicals and goes a long way.

- Buy shampoo and conditioner in bulk.

And of course the BIGGEST money saver is to grow your own garden. Seeds and a bag of soil can cost a few bucks and then grow you $50 worth of produce. For example, you can plant a small strawberry patch that will give you amazingly sweet berries for years and years. A few little strawberry starts can grow into a pretty big patch.

You can grow food in tubs and planters on your apartment patio, pots in the kitchen window. You can even grow food from left over's. When garlic starts growing that little green tail you can stick it in the dirt and grow a ton of it from a little clove. Celery can be re grown from soaking the bottom that you chop off when cutting it up. Potatoes start to grow little branches when we leave them on the counter too long. Chop them up and stick them in the dirt. It really can be that easy!

You can make a game of it, do some research and see just how cheap and easy to can make it and just how much you can plant. It doesn't take that much space or money. I once saw a YouTube video of some poor people in the Philippines that used old milk cartons and food cans to grow their garden in. Some of them only had patios, but they were loaded with vegetables. You can grow an abundance of veggies and berries with limited space and resources and save hundreds of dollars a season. Like Rob Fineley said, "It's like growing money". Have fun with this.

The last grocery tip is to not waste anything.

- Use all the leftovers, either pack in lunches or use leftover meat and veggies for a casserole or soup.

- Even veggie scraps and bones can be simmered for hours to make soup stock.

- Old bananas become banana bread or freeze for smoothies.

- Berries should be frozen for smoothies or baking.

- Old bread can be used for croutons. You get the idea. Waste nothing.

<u>**Learn to cook from scratch**</u>, it's easier than you think and it makes the home more cozy and home like. There is nothing sweeter than a stew simmering on the stove and a couple loaves of homemade bread baking in the oven on a cold winter day. I always felt that cooking and baking made a house a home. It will also save a lot of money.

When you think about eating out, think about how much you would spend and then think about how many groceries you could get and live on with the money you just spent on one dinner. A $40 dinner out on the town equates to 3 full days of groceries, breakfast, lunch and dinner. How's that steak lookin' now?

Chapter 6

Downsize the Royal Garage

How about getting rid of a car...or two? Maybe you only have one car, but live in town. Can you walk to work, maybe bicycle, roller blade, skate board? If you live in town you can walk anywhere, all the time (well, maybe not late at night if in some areas).

Think about downsizing a car. Getting rid of a car payment and the extra insurance and gas will save a bundle. If the car is paid off, selling it can earn some quick cash toward paying off a credit card.

Public transportation can be much cheaper, especially if you get a monthly pass. You can sit on the train, Bart or bus and read, watch a movie on your iPad, have a morning chat with a friend on the cell, dream about your new frugal life. Someone else drives, you have no stress, no accidents, you can just sit back and drink the latte you brought from home and enjoy the view and that good romance book you haven't had time to read. Your blood pressure will go down and think...no more trips to the gas station (I detest pumping gas).

Even if you keep a car, think about ways to not use it and save on gas. Walk to the store with your own bag and be double Green. Walking everywhere, or riding your bike, roller blading or skating is great exercise and a great way to get to discover your neighborhood. You are also doing the Earth a service by reducing pollution. Think you can't make a difference? Many an Empire or Corporation has been taken down by one person. You get out there and walk everywhere and others will see you and it will start to get them thinking. We have a collective conscious and you will see masses of populations start to change with just one person making a small change.

Oregon is well known for having a walking city. Instead of building more highways and adding more lanes, they made smaller streets and more walking and biking paths. This cuts down on the smog, keeps citizens fit and healthy and the area is by far more attractive than a city that becomes all on ramps and freeways. Let's stop making more roads and start planting more trees to walk under!

Chapter 7

Making an Inexpensive Royal Baby

This chapter is for you only if you have a baby coming or in the planning phase. If you already have one, then this chapter is too late.

Babies don't need even half the stuff people get for the precious arrival. After my second son I wound up giving away 3 truckloads of stuff that had barely been used.

It all depends on how extreme you need or want to go and your comfort level. Dial it up or down to fit you.

A tiny 8 pound baby doesn't need its own room in the beginning. It may not even need a crib in the beginning (or ever). Many parents have taken to having the little ones sleep with them. This is normal in most parts of Asia and Europe, only in America do doctors warn against this. Some people are not for this for reasons of wanting spousal intimacy (which doesn't have to be sacrificed, you just have to utilize the family couch or guest room). Some say sleep deprivation. I found it much easier to have my children in our bed and I slept far better, because I nursed them right there, I didn't need to get up and go to another room, nurse, rock them to sleep and then go back to bed, this would be repeated several times in the night. No, I just cuddled, nursed and slept. I also felt that they were safer with me; I would wake up instantly if they had a fever or sudden illness in the night.

Cribs. Sleeping with your babies is a very loving and nurturing thing, babies don't want to sleep alone in a big crib, they want to be snuggled next to their mamma's smelling her scent and hearing her heart beat all night. Think about it, we spend our whole lives trying to find someone to share our bed with, why would a little, new being want to sleep alone in this huge, new world filled with scary sounds and new sights and smells after being wrapped up tight in a warm, dark womb?

Some caution though, it is not safe to sleep with babies if you drink, smoke pot, take any kind of medication that makes you drowsy or sleeping aids. You need to be very sober to sleep safely with a baby.

So, if you decide to sleep with the new wonder, you can save hundreds on a crib that only the cat will use. You can also forget about all the little portable cribs too.

- You can lay them on the bed in the middle for the first few months before they learn to roll over or scoot off things.

- You can also use a large basket if you want a Noah's basket type deal to carry baby from room to room.

- A thick blanket on the floor works great too, unless you have dogs and cats that will bother baby.

By the way, dogs and cats are great for kids. Children with pets have way less allergies and they learn compassion and selflessness in caring for another living being. Dogs can be a little weird when you bring the new bundle home, but once that bundle turns into a toddler with snacks, dogs learn very quick how great this new family member can be after the first time a cheese cracker gets shoved in its snout.

Diaper changing table? Please, what a waste of royal pennies. I place a towel on my freshly made bed every morning. Next to it I put diapers, wipes and whatever else you need. That has been my changing table for years.

Blankets and clothes. Baby showers are great for getting you started. You will probably get almost everything you need to begin. The wise thing to do is have a list of "needs", very different from "wants". Go over that list with the hostess of the party.

Needs:

Car seat
Diapers (specify if you want cloth)
Wipes (you could use wash cloths)
Onesies
Pajamas
Bottles (unless you nurse, but on hand just in case is wise)
Swaddling blankets
Baby blankets

Formula is awful stuff. You can get some that is pretty good, but nursing is the way to go. By nursing you give the baby enzymes and antibodies that they can't get from formula. An amazing immune system is built on mother's milk. An amazing bond is also built from nursing.

I found that nursing solved everything from digestive issues to just being able to comfort my child in an instant. Studies show that nursing makes smarter and more confident babies, that they are much healthier, weather illness quicker and easier. The list of benefits goes on. Do some research on the web. Nursing is also free and you don't have to wash bottles or pack anything when going out. Handy! However, sometimes a mother just can't nurse for many reasons. Have no fear; there are good formulas out there. Goat milk with added vitamins and minerals is a great way to go. Please consult a knowledgeable Pediatrician or Naturopathic DC.

Diapers. You can go with cloth and save a bundle. Cloth is a bit of a commitment, I tried it and only lasted a few months. Do a little research to make sure you wash and use them properly. It's great environmentally and for the purse, but you need to wash them a certain way and use certain detergents so as not to cause diaper rash. Definitely talk to a fellow cloth diaper mom to learn the tricks to make it painless. If you go with the disposable diapers that's understandable, but there are ways to make that box last a lot longer. Today's diapers have a wicking clothe and are made to hold up to 10 lbs. of liquid. No matter how wet the diaper is the baby stays dry. So, let that diaper fill up before you change it. I would not recommend the 10 lb. limit, but don't change the diaper after every pee, or 2 or 3.   If you have cloth you do have to change after every single pee.

Wipes. You can go with the disposable or you can make your own (on the internet will be a recipe). You can also use a wash cloth with good old fashioned warm water and soap. You can buy a big stack of cheap wash clothes at the thrift store. You will need a lot of them. If you are going with cloth diapers and wash clothes you will save about $60 plus a month.

Clothes. Whatever you don't get at the baby shower, go to the local thrift shops. I bought tons of the cutest clothes at Goodwill for a few dollars. Baby clothes are stained and ruined and out grown at the blink of an eye. A dollar for an outfit is smart. Don't spend $25 on an outfit that will be worn twice. Thrift stores are great for toys too. Just make sure and soak in hot water and soap when you bring home or wash in a hot wash in the washing machine and a hot dryer if it's a washable item.

Blankets. You can make your own if you crochet or put grandma to work. These will also come at the baby shower and you really only need a few.

Toys and rattles. Let me tell you this, kids will spend more time playing with the empty box the toy was delivered in than the toy itself sometimes. They don't need any toys in the beginning, just you and the wide world, some sunshine, dirt and music. That will keep them busy for many, many months. After that a few toys are fun (mostly for you). I created drawers in the kitchen that were "baby drawers". They had all the Tupper ware and wooden spoons, baby dishes and safe stuff for them to dig through and play. Baby just wants to be near you and loves to play in the drawers and pull everything out and bang on things.

Baby dishes. All they need are plastic (get BPA free) dishes, bowls and cups. They can use the adult, just as long as it's plastic. What they do need are small spoons and sippy cups in later months.

Baby food. Invest in a Cuisinart (you can find one online with eBay or at a thrift store or see if a friend is getting rid of an extra). Take regular food, squash, sweet potatoes, carrots and such, steam and puree! Bananas and avocados are great smashed and you can make your own apple sauce very easily. Much easier than you think.

So, there you have it. Babies are not that expensive, it's when they start walking and talking that it gets a bit pricy. But even then you can be thrifty.

Children DO need:

- Tons of love (free)
- Great nutrition
- A lot of outdoor play, sunshine, clean dirt, exercise and their beautiful imaginations.

Children DON'T need:

- iPads and iPods and cell phones. A few recent studies by the Pediatric Association says that hand held devices should not be introduced to a child until the age of 12. The devices and too much TV interrupts brain function and development, causes visual problems and children who spend too much time with hand held devices, computer games and TV lack imagination, they don't learn skills in problem solving, being creative, building friendships and so much more. You are actually crippling the child with these toys. Even Steve Jobs once said, in an interview, that his children were not allowed iPads/iPods because he knew what it does to a person. Scary right?
- Too much TV. Kills a child's learned ability to be creative and imaginative.
- Video games. Also causes problems with brain development and growth.
- Expensive toys and gadgets.

  All those expensive toys and gadgets aren't good for a child's growth and development.

All the free stuff, parks, rivers, forest, fun with mom and dad...that is what is going to build an amazing child and family.

Have fun, being a mother has been the best career move I ever made.

Chapter 8

Royal Beauty

Being royal means that you have to keep up some appearances right? I am a stay at home Queen mother, however I enjoy going out among the people now and then and I must look my best.

As a woman I, personally, feel that it is very important for us to groom and preen. For our self-esteem and as an expression of self-love and honor, we must take excellent care of ourselves. Love yourself, look your best and take care of what God blessed you with.

Clothes. Yes, you guessed it. The thrift store is your BFF. I have created and recreated a few new wardrobes for under a hundred bucks many times. You will find fabulous name brand items at the local thrift if you really take the time to look through all the racks. I have purchased Jones of New York, J. Jill and many other fancy brands I can't remember for $5 when I know that in the store it would have cost in the hundreds new.

You go when you have lots of time to look and don't be turned off by the rows and rows of old cloths. There are gems in there. You can create whatever look you desire for dollars. You can find quality and pieces that are almost new. Try all the thrift stores in your area. You may hate one and fall in love with another.

Cosmetics. I find some cosmetics at discount stores and outlets. I also buy my hair dye there for half the cost. Your local drug store will have Maybelline and L'Oréal and such. These brands are just as good as going to a cosmetic counter at a department store. I used to work as a cosmetics girl and L'Oréal is the step child of Lancôme. Getting all your beauty stuff at a local drug store will save a load and be just as good.

Hair. I dye my own hair. There are so many great dyes out there now. You can even get frosting kits. Anyone can do it without a license. If you are doing a fancy frosting, you may want a friend to help. Doing your own hair will look just as fabulous as a saloon and cost $6 to $10 as opposed to $150.

You can even trim your own hair. I've found do it yourself YouTube videos on how to trim bangs and do bobs! However, I would suggest either a friend who you can do trade with or finding a salon that is not that expensive, but gives great haircuts. I spend no more than $25 to $35 plus tip and I get my hair a little extra short so I can spread out my visits. Choose a hair style that is sheik and that grows out well.

Dieting. First off I will say that I'm totally opposed to dieting. Dieting makes one fat. The junk food and fast food and all that processed, prepackaged food makes you fat. I started dieting at 11 years old and went from a slim kid to a chubby gal over the years. When I became pregnant I couldn't diet and fast anymore and what a feeling of freedom that was! I have never dieted again. Even thinking about it makes me gain weight.

When you start eating clean, home cooked meals and walking everywhere you will slim down if you need to. Naturally.

With all that said if you are one of those people that loves to diet than here are some cheap alternatives:

Jenny Craig is very popular and very expensive. You can create your own home made Jenny by shopping for all the mix and match frozen and boxed meals in stores now. Lean Cuisine and Weight Watchers have all the breakfast, lunch and dinners, desserts and snacks. Just create your own meal plans. Jenny Craig cost around $400 to $600 and you can do it yourself for half the cost, especially if you follow the sales and buy 2 for 1 deals.

Weight Watchers is cheap and you can do it at home and not buy the meals, but make your own. If you are eating clean and homemade this is the best program for you. You can cook for you and the family without any inconvenience. You will also have a support group and meeting weekly. This is helpful.

And then there are the millions of other diets out there, Paleo, Adkins, fat free, no sugar or flour. It goes on and they are all free to try. I say just dump the junk and get outside and walk.

GYMS. If you have a garage or extra room not being utilized, you can get some great work out equipment at discount retailers or online. People are always selling their used equipment. Ditch the gym membership and create one at home with a used treadmill and weight machine.

If you have very little space, just get some free weights and walking shoes. I do a whole body work out with my free weights while watching my favorite sitcom. You can also invest in work out DVD's. You can do yoga, Zumba, step and weight training right in your living room.

So, there you have it. You can even take care of the bode and look amazing on a budget.

Chapter 9

Having Fun is Priceless

There are times when we need a little something extra or different to run our earth ship or we need to tweak a thing or two to be happier, feel more satisfied, and make our lives fuller. Life must be made fun and joy filled. This is a priority for health and happiness.

Being frugal can sometimes feel like all we do is save, pinch, refrain, stop, don't do it, don't buy it, don't give in to "it" (whatever the it may be, chocolate, new clothes, toys for the children). There can be a lot of giving things up because the only way to be truly frugal is to always ask the million dollar question, "Do I really need this?" It gets old after a while.

So, this chapter is all about what you *can* have in your new frugal life. Let's start with entertainment. What can you and your family do without opening the wallet? The answer is, lots of things!

Libraries. Love that library, it will become your Barnes and Noble, your Block Buster and so much more. You can order all kinds of movies (warning: they may take a while to arrive, especially if new and popular), you can order books of all kinds from all over the state once you become savvy to how to order, I believe you can even find magazines and music. How great is that? Most libraries have story time for the little ones and a children's section with toys and learning tools and computers. My boys play for hours at our library.

Parks are a combination of nature and amusement parks. Well, maybe not amusement parks, but kids love parks and it gives them a social life and lots of exercise, fresh air and sun. We go almost daily. I pack a mini picnic and ice water, sometimes coffee for me if we go in the morning. We meet all kinds of interesting and fun people and have a great time. The kids come home tired and peaceful and I get a chance to have me time. A friend once said, when I got a new dog, "a tired puppy is a good puppy". This is true of children and adults too.

Community centers are great resources for classes and family fun.

Look up online local activities that are free. Free concerts in the park, free movies in the park, most walk and run events can be free too.

Church, Buddhist centers, temples, synagogues. These are great places to make friends that are like minded, join a community and be a part of a group. I strongly advocate a spiritual practice of some kind for sanity, faith, joy and strength. You can also do volunteer work through these centers or have your children join youth groups, summer camps and missionary work. Missionary work offers travel, community, being a part of the solution, doing good works in the world with our brothers and sisters and mother earth, learning compassion and service.

Churches also have bible studies and choir groups. If you want to educate yourself or have musical talent you want to share you can join. There are support groups and men's and women's groups also to bring about togetherness and bonding. A church or spiritual center can be a wonderful thing to be a part of with so many activities for you and everyone in your family. Spiritual centers also offer all kinds of classes for enrichment and healing. I have done some major healing and self-improvement through classes offered at The Center for Spiritual Living (the church of my choice).

That brings us to volunteer work. You can do this through a church or just a community based center. There are all kinds of volunteer work from feeding others to planting trees, community gardens and so much more! You can even travel if that is possible for you. This kind of work is fun, feeds the soul and gives back to the community you live in. It also makes you a part of something bigger than yourself. If you ever want to get away from your problems or get out of a funk, join a group, a soup kitchen or mission.

These are some of the really big forms of entertainment and/or self-improvement that can be done for cheap to no cost.

Some of the extra fun and inexpensive things you can do as a family or single person are:

- Go to McDonalds for a $1 coffee and the kids can play in the Play land.

- Some theaters offer a cheap Tuesday or day that they charge only a few dollars.

- Have a pot luck at your house. If organized properly, you will only have to provide one dish and the ware to eat it on.

- Have a pot luck and bar b q at the park. Make sure you organize what everyone brings so you don't get stuck with all the coals and meat and sodas.

- Go to the thrift store as a treat or reward to a child and let them pick out a few items. After all, everything is cheap.

- Stock up on art supplies at a discount store. You can get big boxes of crayons and coloring books pennies. Art supplies may not be of the best quality, but when children are little all they do is eat and break crayons anyway. You can also get tons of playdough that kids go through like crazy.

- Make your own playdough. You just need cream of tartar, flour, salt, oil and food coloring. Kids love to make this and it last for a long time. You'll find a recipe online.

- Have a friend or two over for coffee and have one of them bring the scones or make a batch from scratch.

- Change up your wardrobe or completely recreate it. Allot yourself a budget and go to several thrift stores. Make a day of it. Create 5 outfits you can mix and match.

- Go to a Nordstrom's or Macy's and have one of the cosmetic ladies give you a complete makeover for free. I suggest you buy at least one item so you don't get a reputation as a customer that is just there for the freebies. Sometimes they will give you samples, but last I checked they were getting pretty stingy. Cosmetic counters have what they call "Gift with Purchase". If you time it right, you can get in on this and get your make over and a gift with just one purchase. Fun, fun, fun!

- Sometimes just going to the mall and wandering around can be fun. We go to the indoor malls and treat ourselves to a couple pieces of See's candy. They always give out samples so you really don't need that many treats. I get the kids lollipops because it'll last them a whole day to eat.

- Go to markets where they are known to have samples. You can try all kinds of yummies you wouldn't normally eat and basically have a free hors d'oeuvres.

- Get a good antenna and put it on the roof to get all the local FREE channels.

- Radio is free music all day long!

- Farmers market is very fun and you can get your local, inexpensive produce for the week.

- Public pools are inexpensive and wonderful for hot days. I try to go when it's not so busy, like the middle of the week.

- I read a lot for fun and I love to write.

- Blogging. Many people do this for fun and to share advice and experiences.

- Research on the web. I enjoy watching YouTube or reading blogs from women who are also housewives and stay at home moms. I get great ideas and advice that has served to improve my budget, the way I clean, new recipes, being better with my sons, gardening on the cheap and so much more.

- Calling friends and family. We have Vonage and it is a flat rate of around $37 a month local and long distance. My husband calls India all the time, so this is a great deal. I love having some down time and catching up with a friend in Oregon or my auntie on the coast. Talking on the phone is a lost art and must be revived.

- Send letters and cards the old fashioned way. I send cards I collect from many of the charities I support. When you support a charity, some of them send cards and envelopes you can save and use, they send address labels and calendars and all kinds of goodies. I save and use it all.

- Send a letter with a drawing your child made or photos of the family, even a hand written recipe. People love getting these presents in the mail, because it really is a lost art...that also needs revivin'.

- For autumn fun go to the local farms and pick pumpkins, ride tractors and eat kettle corn and hot chocolate.

- Decorate the house for all the seasons and holidays. Kids love this and it is very festive year round. You can start collecting decorations from the thrift stores for pennies and even some things at the Dollar store. For fall we purchase pumpkins at the farms to decorate inside and outside. When done with pumpkins you can toast the seeds and cook up the pumpkins for the dogs. Pumpkin is great for their digestive tract. You can also make pumpkin soup, breads and pies depending on what kind of pumpkin you collected.

- Knit or crochet. Teach yourself or see if there are local classes. I made blankets for both my sons. I have not gone beyond squares, but I enjoy crocheting while watching a good Hallmark movie.

- Make tons of popcorn and a do family movie night. In place of soda I do ice water with a splash of cranberry juice. You can make several bowls of popcorn and use different herbs, nutritional yeast, and powdered cheese and so on to make each bowl a different flavor.

- Spring or fall cleaning. Can be fun, but mostly it is for the soul. Crank up the music, brew some tea or coffee or a big pitcher of lemonade and get going. Scrubbing the house room by room from beam to board feels so good after. Add to that a box to put "thrift donations" and a garbage bag for junk and really clean everything out and scrub. This gives the house a shine and fresh and balanced feel and will give you a feel of accomplishment and peace from having the house organized again.

- Go back to school or just take a class through the community college. Want to start over? Want to start or change careers? Maybe you just want to learn how to write screen plays or how to speak fluent French. The community college has classes for getting certificate, a trade or transferring for a degree. You can get BOG fee waivers to pay for your classes and even financial aid for books and parking passes. When you are a low income family there is a lot of help out there if you do the research and work.

- Write a book.

- Do a how to on YouTube.

- Learn to sew or if you do, make some clothes or do a quilt.

- Learn new recipes.

- Bake bread from scratch. In the fall and winter we bake cakes and breads weekly. It's great for kids to learn how to cook and clean up and the stove adds extra heat to the house when it's chilly. There is nothing like fresh, hot bread with butter and honey or jam.

- Bake a cake from scratch, frosting and all.

- Learn crafts, scrap booking or make a dream board from old magazines.

- Learn to meditate daily. You could even set up a space in your home to meditate with candles, pillows and whatever you want to make a peaceful space.

- Build a garden and plant food year round.

- See how many herbs you can grow in your kitchen.

- Have a garage or yard sale. Invite some friends to do it with you. Bake brownies and make lemonade to put out for the event. Make it fun. Great way to make some money.

- Rearrange a room or a few in your house. Have a friend help that's good at this sort of thing (unless you work better alone). It's almost like having a new living room if you really get into it.

- Paint a room a new color. If it turns out well, paint all your rooms.

- Recreate your front yard or patio.

- Repaint some furniture. I had an old dresser I almost threw out. I spray painted it a bold cherry red and it looked fabulous.

- Play board games or cards with the family. You can buy cheap games at all thrift stores. Just make sure all the pieces are in there.

- Walk your dog...or the neighbors. Wow, what a treat that will be for the neighbor and their dog!

- Create a free home gym. Yoga, free weights, jogging, walking daily or get some work out DVD's. You can also find used treadmills and weight machines on places like craigslist.

- Have a picnic at the park.

- Start or join a book club.

- Start your own self-help group. You can study spiritual books and do steps toward inner healing and self-exploration. This could become a therapy group. Make tea and have someone in charge of goodies each week or month.

- Make Sunday pancakes.

- Put a stack of paper, coloring books and a jar of crayons, pencils and pens on the table and leave it there so the little people can do artwork whenever inspired.

- Always have batches of play dough ready.

- Go to high school sporting events and plays. They are much cheaper than the big city events.

- Talk to yourself. I do this often being that I spend a lot of time alone and with little people. I can talk about anything I choose and a great length without boring anyone. I've done therapy this way and I swear, as crazy as it sounds, it works. Just don't let anyone catch you.

- Let you kids do your make up.

- Play dress up with your kids.

- Sit down and color with them.

- Spend weekends going to garage sales. Bring homemade muffins and a thermos of coffee.

- Try a new radio station.

Chapter 10

Decorating the Castle...or Cottage

Decorating on a budget can be very fun. I believe it to be more fun than if you have all kinds of disposable income and can just wily nilly buy whatever. When on a budget you have to plan, search, make wish list, save pictures from magazines, create a dream board...not really. You can and that is fun to, but I just love to go to all the thrift stores and garage sales and find all kinds of treasures and create a home that is very personalized.

Be so very grateful that you are blessed with a home and show that appreciation by making it the best you can. Even if you are living in an undesirable neighborhood in a tiny box with a tiny patio...you can make it amazing for pennies. Challenge yourself, be creative. It is your family's sanctuary and an expression of you and your family. It is also very important for your children to have a home that they are proud of and has balance, harmony and is organized and clean to create a feeling of peacefulness.

I have decorated a few apartments and studios from Goodwill and yard sales. I created and built a daycare from craigslist and thrift stores. I don't suggest mattresses or couches though. I only get things I can scrub or throw in the washer on hot. I may get a used couch if it's from a friend and I know the life it's had. Same goes for a mattress if it was just a guest room bed and hardly used.

You can get almost everything you need to create a home from craigslist, thrift stores, Goodwill, Salvation Army, local garage sales, even some antique stores will have a deal or two. If you're feeling really lucky you can play the "get it free" game. There are free, recycling and trading sites on line in most areas. Now, there are all kinds of frugal and fun ways to create or recreate your house, from studios to a home you own. You may have these things or just be starting out. Perhaps you just want to change things. Let's go room by room.

The Living Room

A few nice area rugs, lots of plants and a few nice paintings and it's a home! I suggest having a plain couch with lots of colorful pillows. If the couch is ratty shed no tears, an inexpensive slip cover can make it like new. You can get some really nice faux suede slip covers that have a separate cover for the seat cushions and a big slip for the rest of the couch. I love these kinds because they stay put when you sit and roll about without having to adjust constantly and don't look like a sheet thrown over it. It looks like the couch was re upholstered. The best part is that if you tire of the color you can interchange with another slip cover. You can also get slip covers for tired arm chairs and recliners. If you need to go cheaper, you can cover the couch with a quilt or nice blanket.

A big book case or entertainment center with shelves is crucial. You can fill it up with books and plants and candles and it makes the living room very cozy.

For a coffee table you can get a used one or use an ottoman with a piece of glass or wood on top. A big, old chest is charming.

You can get house plants for cheap by getting some starts from a friend. Ivy type plants just need to be trimmed off a plant and put in a glass of water in the window until it takes root and then plant in a pot. You can buy plane pots for cents and then paint them or find other ways to decorate. Just buy some old salad plates and put under the plant pots. A bag of potting soil can be a few dollars. You can also find free soil, pots and even plants on swaps and craigslist sometimes.

Kitchen

You can get a lot of pots and pans and utensils at thrift stores; however, don't buy any nonstick pans. If you can find cast iron, you have scored! Cast iron pots and pans are what our grandmothers used for nonstick. They last forever to infinite and work great if treated and you get the benefit of some iron in your diet. Cast iron pans just need to be seasoned properly to work fabulously. You'll want to scrub with a wire pad and get all the crust and rust off, wash well and then grease inside and out liberally and bake in the oven for an hour. Sometimes you need to bake a couple times to set. Once it's seasoned do not ever use soap on it. You will have the best and healthiest nonstick pan ever.

Kitchens need character. My kitchen is my favorite room. I cook all my meals for my family I love, I bake bread and cakes from scratch, I brew my beloved morning coffee and I do therapy with friends over tea and scones at our kitchen nook. Not to mention the Christmas baking and Thanksgiving turkeys. Kitchens are the heart of a home.

Start with a washable rug to throw in front of the sink to add color to the floor. Create a coffee station on the counter where you have the pot, tin of coffee, a creamer and sugar bowl, put a scented candle near it. I love to light my candle early in the morning and make my cup of coffee. Little touches make little moments sweet.

Next, have some herb plants in the window or on the counter. Create an herb garden where ever you can. Fresh herbs for cooking are yummy and it freshens up the room with the scents and greenery. For storage you can find containers at the thrift store. They don't have to match. Or you can use large mason jars. I fill them with what I use most like flour, rice, beans, sugar, coffee and so on. I love the mason jars, because they are clear and I can see what I have and it looks colorful on the counter. Fill a pitcher or jar with often used cooking utensils near the stove. I always have a couple chopping boards on the counter ready to work. One is wood for bread, fruit and veggies. The other is plastic for garlic, onions and meat. Plastic you can bleach to clean meat residue or stinky onion and garlic.

A couple pictures on the walls and I usually put frequently used baking recipes and photos on the front of my cupboards. Sounds strange but I love the look. I can just read the bread recipe on the front of a cabinet or see a picture that makes me happy of my babies. On the frig I have all kinds of fun magnets from trips and photos of loved ones, I have the list of the Dirty Dozen and Clean Fifteen for organic shopping. Decorate with whatever is related to cooking and family. Make this a happy space that you want to be in and create yummy dishes and snacks.

Bedrooms

Bedrooms are not just for catching some z's. We take afternoon naps, lie on the bed and read that juicy novel; some of us have a little desk and computer for doing some work and so much more.

Have a great area rug, maybe a little rug on either side of the bed. Plants and candles, a painting or family photos on the walls. Utilize the closet with a shelving unit and I suggest baskets for storage. Design the room for what you use it for. If you need a little work space, get a little desk and lamp and make it aesthetically pleasing and efficient.

Guest rooms just need a bed and dresser, a night table and lamp. I always put my extra photos and paintings in this room instead of storing them. I would have a plant on the dresser with some scented lotion and tissue. When I had guest I would pick a bouquet of my home grown flowers for the night table. Create a bed and breakfast scene so your guest enjoys being there and they have their own space. If you don't have a guest room, try to have a pull out couch or day bed in the living room. We all have guest at one time or another. Air mattress's work great too.

Kid's rooms need to have their personalities all over them. Have your child(ren) help with creating their room. If you have more children than rooms, you can use bunk beds and you'll need to create storage in the closet. Tubs, baskets and crates stacked make great storage. There are bunk beds with desk built in and drawers that save lots of room. IKEA has great ideas for storage efficient furniture. I look in magazines to get ideas and then create something with what I have or a less expensive version.

Kids love to paint their room so have them choose a fun color and go for it. You can also get decals that stick on windows and even walls that won't ruin the paint or glass. A big trunk or huge baskets or tubs for throwing toys in and a book shelf. You can get a shelving unit for free and then paint it. If you have little ones, please bolt it to the wall. Little ones like to climb things to get favorite toys and books. Fill the shelves up with books and toys. Load the beds up with colorful pillows and stuffed toys. Put some photos of them in there, photos of them playing and having fun.

Bathroom

Colorful bathroom rugs and a great shower curtain can make a huge difference. You can get these items at discount stores. Use a big basket for laundry, a basket for rolled up towels and wash cloths. Put a basket on the sink filled with soap, lotion and hair brushes. A simple jar or cup can be used for tooth brushes and tooth paste.

The Yard

With some potting soil, seeds, starts and lots of imagination you can do all kinds of things to your yard or patio.   With some hunting and scavenging you can get all kinds of things for free or cheap. Online you can find Freecycle or craigslist or whatever is available in your area.

- You can get dirt, manure, pots, even plants and trees for free. People need to just get rid of the very thing you may need.

- Some towns have electric and gas companies that will actually give you free trees. Look into it.

- Another thing that you can easily find for free is lumber. You could build your own raised beds. All you need are 4 pieces of lumber, a saw and with some dirt and manure you have the starts of a garden.

- You can create your own free and rich fertilizer with composting.

Composting is very easy. All you need is a small space and you just throw all the left over fruits and veggies, leaves, grass trimmings and some dirt in a pile and cover. Egg shells and coffee grounds are good too. No dairy or meat or other cooked foods, especially processed or fruit in sugar juice, veggies in gravy. You can cover with a tarp if you like. Every couple months you take a pitch fork and turn it all over and mix it up. Within 6 months to a year you will have dark soil at the bottom.

Nothing has to be complicated. Figure out what zone you are for gardening. Online you just look up your area and ask what agricultural zone you are classified as. Then you can find a gardener's calendar and see what you can plant year round.

There is a list of books I have added to the back of this book and one is about gardening. There are all kinds of advice for pest control and soil maintenance and do it yourself stuff. You can get this book and many other beginning gardener books at the library.

Plants and vines can transform a yard or house and all you have to do is keep trimming off the mother plant and root and transplant.

Have fun and really put time and thought in how to customize your home. Set up sanctuaries, blow up family photos and frame for the walls, do some of your own art. Make your castle so cozy and inviting.

The biggest thing you can do is take pride in your home, keep it clean and tidy and every once in a while rearrange the furniture or do a touch up, paint a room or add curtains.

Chapter 11

Staying Home

A big decision some households make, that propels the whole frugal movement, is to have one of the partners stay home. Perhaps you are having a wee one and want to be a stay at home mother or father. Perhaps one of you is miserable in your line of work, maybe you want to return to school, create a home business or maybe one of you just wants to be home creating the nest.

Traditionally the woman was expected to stay home when she married. That was encouraged and just how things were supposed to happen. Now a days it seems to be sort of looked down upon. It seems that the right to stay home as a house wife or house husband has to be explained, even defended. I feel like the house wife is a dying breed...and yet, I also feel like it's an old trend becoming popular again. The housewife position is having a revival!

I love, love, love being a housewife, however I have also created some outside interest such as classes, volunteer work and even becoming a part owner at the Co-op I shop. There are so many things we do as a family such as traveling, weekly trips to the library, daily trips to various parks, attending workshops, spending time with friends and extended family.

Being a housewife can be very enjoyable and VERY economical. If you are giving up a large commute, you save on all the commute fair or all the gas and car maintenance. If you live in town you can even get rid of that car and bike, walk or bus everywhere and get rid of a car payment and insurance. That's hundreds saved in a month right there. If you need to keep the extra car you will still save plenty on gas and become more environmentally friendly.

Then there are the lunches out, lattes before you get to the office, the work clothes you must buy. If you have children, there is the daycare cost. It can all add up to thousands. How much are you making after you pay out everything it cost to work?

What if you aren't paying out much and these list do nothing to support the consideration of staying home.   Well, there are plenty of reasons why having one person stay home is still a great idea!

 If you are a truly great nester and enjoy cooking and cleaning and running a home, you should have this job.

Food for thought.   People who are very busy and can afford it, hire and pay others to do their home chores.

- People get paid to clean houses, sometimes they are actually hired full time to keep a house clean and tidy.

- People are paid to do all the menu planning, shopping and cooking.

- How about the person hired to drive the kids to school and activities and to drive the family on outings and errands?

- People are paid to do the gardening, to mow the lawn and weed and prune the trees.

- There is the person paid to walk Fido.

- Some people are even paid just to grocery shop!

All the things a house wife does all day long for free (well not really for free). There are people out there getting paid to do it. So, if someone ignorant says that you aren't working, you laugh and do your best sarcastic teenage, "whatever!".   And if you have children, don't forget that there are nannies and baby sitters and day cares that get paid to do that also.

I can't even tell you the extent of how beneficial and positive it is for a family or even just a couple to have one person tend to the home.

- You keep the home clean and organized and running smooth.

- You take care of all the bills and administration aspect such as medical, dental, appointments, DMV, school activities or home schooling and so on.

- You can have the time to plan, shop and cook healthy foods for your loved ones.

- You have can grow an organic garden to feed your family and save hundreds of dollars' year round.

- There will be someone to walk the poor dog and love on him instead of the mutt being home alone all day. Yes, even the pets benefit from your presence. Everyone loves having mom or dad around.

My biggest advice would be to only do it if you really love being home and being busy tending to the needs of your family or just the partner. You need to love cooking and cleaning and be organized and efficient. You must be able to multi task. Yes, ladies and gentlemen, it is a job and you need to get up, have that cup of coffee and clock in just like you would at a job.

It would be very unfair to have one partner go to work and fight the commute, deal with a boss and the stress of keeping a position while the other stays home to lay about and watch soap operas. That is not what it's about. It is about you or the mate choosing to stay at home to run the home ship and being a partner and companion that supports the other by running the household. One person goes out to work and the other stays home to work.

The other money savings that come with being at home are planting a garden, be it an apartment patio garden or a big back yard garden, heck, some people are planting front yard gardens now instead of silly lawns. You can have an abundance of organic veggies and berries for pennies in the cost of seeds. You can have produce year round! Yay! You could even go crazy with farm fever and have chickens and then you'd have eggs year round (except when they are molting). Woowie!

Staying home means you can plan those meals and that is budget friendly. Cooking all meals, snacks and drinks at home is also very budget friendly. We have spent almost a week's worth of grocery money on one crappy meal out.

You can mend and sew old clothes back to life instead of buy new, you could even make your own clothes and quilts. I'm not this handy yet, but I did get the sewing machine for when that crafty talent kicks in.

The pets will love you, you can play with them, take them for walks, social time at the dog park. The cat won't need much and will let you know when she does, until then just stay out of her way.

Your partner will have coffee sent with him on the commute and lunch packed and that is savings of money and health. Eating out is not good for the heart or waste line.

You can tend to your own child(ren) and save on daycare or preschool. Later or now you can home school and that can save a huge bundle. No class photos, uniforms or trendy school clothes, school lunches (that is reason enough to take the kids out of school), sports cost (although I support getting them into sports and such outside of school no matter what).

You have time to rummage garage sales, thrift stores or online swaps and free cycles for whatever your family and home need.

You can sit and make a long list of all the pluses to staying home. The only negative would be if you really didn't want to. If you are in debt right now and need the two incomes, this gives you a goal to work toward. Save and work hard to pay off all the debt so you can experience freedom and choices you just don't have with debt looming.

Although, some people find that one person staying home actually helps to tackle the debt because, for example, let's say the wife's income wasn't much and with her home it's saving a little. People don't realize how much it really cost to have both people working. Not just in money but in health and sanity. It's hard to work a 40 to 60 hour week with commuting and then try and clean, shop, yard work and all the house stuff on the two days off. With kids and pets, it's even harder to do all the cooking and homework, walking the dog, laundry and on and on everyday along with commuting and working.

This is not living. People wind up eating out a lot more than they realize because they are exhausted. They pay for a dog walker and house keeper and gardener. And you should if you are busy, but if funds are tight, this is another stressor.

So, to simplify your life, save money and bring balance and harmony to your home, this is a big subject to bring to the table for some discussion.

Homeschooling

If we are on the path to having a parent stay home and reconfiguring life for simplicity and joy, we should discuss schooling options for now or the future. I bring this up, because sometimes this is a big reason that one parent chooses to stay home. People choose to home school for so many reasons. It has become very big in the United States and other countries and grows 10% every year. The modern home schooling movement started in 1970's with a few hundred and now there are over 2 million home schooled students.

Home schooling doesn't have to cost a penny; you utilize the internet and library to the fullest. Of course this depends on what style of teaching and what program you choose. You can home school through a private school and that will cost. If you choose to go through your public school or charter, they will supply the materials. There is the Classic style, Thomas

Jefferson, Waldorf, Montessori, Unschooling (free), and Free Range schooling. There are some others I'm forgetting.

It is important to do a lot of research about this before you decide. It could be the greatest choice you make as a family or be a stressful disaster. I read 30 books on the subject and did all kinds of research through the internet, library and talking to those families actually doing it years before my eldest is even of kindergarten age.

The more I learned the more I felt like it was a great thing for my boys. It is very personal and if you don't go in knowledgeable and prepared you may choose the wrong program for all of you and hate it. That is the key to success, choosing the way to home school that works for your little person or peoples. Also, relax! Make it fun and explore everything until something clicks for all of you.

The pros of home schooling are many and as you do the research you will learn that. Many children benefit and thrive in a safe, nurturing environment that encourages their passions and is led by their interest. Learning should be fun and exciting, not dull and filled with hours of lectures and test. But maybe you have an amazing school? Inspiring teachers? Your children love going to school and are thriving? Then stay with it. If it works, why change it? This is just for those of you questioning traditional schooling and if there is another way. Home schooling is so popular now that I doubt anyone reading this hasn't come across this subject at least once.

All your questions of socialization and sports and being prepared for life and college...that will all be answered when you do the research. Read others experiences and they will tell you everything you want to know. Also, there are co-ops for home schooling families and support groups everywhere now.

Chapter 12

Royal Holidays

Oh, how those holidays cause so much stress and fret. Holidays should be fun and filled with laughter, music, fun and good cheer! Let's get that back! But that means taking it back from our mindset of consumerism.

Holidays were NEVER meant to be about buy, buy, buy or spend, spend, spend. They were NEVER about getting every one of the 50 members of your family everything they wanted on their wish list.

Holidays were about old folklore, creating celebration that would bring families together, magic, music and feasting. The corporations have turned it into a buying frenzy that helps them meet their quarterly quota. Don't buy it!

Tips: Here are a couple tips to get you started.

- First, start a holiday envelope that you put money toward every month just like all the other bills.

- Start shopping for the holiday right after the holiday. Sales are crazy good right after a Christmas or Thanksgiving because the retailer needs to get rid of the left overs. You can save up to 80% sometimes. So, buy the turkey, the canned cranberries, the stuffing and store it (this is where it pays to have a deep freezer). You can even get an extra turkey or two and give to a neighbor less fortunate or elder on a penchant.

- For after Christmas sales you can buy the decorations, the lights, even some basic gift ideas and stock up on baking supplies.

Now, I'm not saying to go out on Black Fridays, that's just nuts. I'm talking a few days after the holiday when everyone is back at work, the madness is over and the streets are quiet. You can sneak into the stores and reap the real benefits.

Thanksgiving. This holiday is easy. If you get invited somewhere then the pressure is off, you can just bring a dish or two. If you do the feast at your house, then you need to think ahead. You provide the turkey and assign dishes and rolls to everyone invited.

The great thing about having it at your house is that you will have tons of left overs, yummy! And don't get me started on frugal things you can do with left overs.

Ok, I'll tell you.

- With the remaining turkey you can make meat pies, soup, casseroles and freeze them.

Boil the carcass (sounds sort of gross right?) and make soup stock and freeze that too.

Christmas. This is the holiday that causes the stress and hand wringing, but if you have saved for it, took advantage of the sales last year (or you will this year because you know now), it won't be so bad. It should be your favorite holiday!

Here is another chance to do a potluck type dinner. Or you and your family can end all the stress and do something wonderful for the community and volunteer at a soup kitchen or homeless shelter. You need to sign up ahead of time though, turns out that everyone has this idea at the holidays.

Or invite a bunch of people over that are far from their families and would be alone during this time. You will have a great time and bring each other joy and comfort.

As for gifts, suggest a secret Santa where everyone draws a name and put a limit on the spending. That way you only have one person to buy for and a small price.

We have little boys and they are the only ones I splurge on. I may collect thrift store items through the year that are really good and in great shape. Or I purchase toys on sale through the year. I love spoiling them during Christmas. They are little and fun and Christmas should really only be spent on the little people.

Baking. As for everyone else, I bake. Christmas is about baking and it is fun for me and fun for the kids and our home smells like sugar cookies for weeks. We decorate by hand and I even let the oldest decorate some of the cookies. I purchase tins and baskets at thrift stores, fill them with our home made sweets. We pass these out to neighbors, friends, family and even our local street dwellers. Don't forget a tin for the mail lady/man, your doctor, dentist and local grocer.

Homemade Gifting. You can also make gifts, crotchet or knit scarves, blankets, hats. Make candles or homemade bath salts. You can make dried baking or soup packages in mason jars. There are so many clever things to do. Get on the ol' internet for ideas. Everyone loves homemade gifts. You put time and energy into it and that says love.

You can get boxes of cards cheap at the discount stores and send these out a couple weeks prior to Christmas. People love getting cards. Add a family photo or letter to the card.

Don't forget to decorate and hang the lights and play those Christmas carols. That is what I love about Christmas. The lights, music, baking.

If you belong to a Church there will be lots of music, plays and activities, maybe even a Church holiday potluck. Do it all, celebrate, get out there!

If you have children, remember, this holiday is really for them. Set aside your own issues (if you have any) and really make it special for them so they can look back on their memories and smile.

All other holidays. All the other holidays are easy compared to those two.

Easter can be done at Church or with a potluck at home, you provide the ham.

Valentine's day you may need to get some cards at the discount store for your children's school. Or better yet, have them make the cards by hand. This teaches them to be thrifty and creative and those cards will have so much value for being hand made.

Halloween you can create costumes with the sewing machine collecting dust and buy cheap candy for all the trick or treaters. Or better yet pass out fresh fruit or healthy, sugar free cookies that you and the children make together. Make fun Halloween foods for dinner and watch scary movies. Maybe choose Disney

Halloween if you have tiny humans. Don't ever show children a movie with violence and gore.

Depending on your culture and religious preference, you may have other holidays and celebrations. Enjoy and embrace them all.

Decorate, Decorate, And Decorate. This is really the foundation of all holidays. Decorate for all of them. You can get cheap decorations at thrift stores. You can make decorations.

I have decorations for all the seasons too. For fall I go to the local farms and get cheap pumpkins and decorate my stoop and house. The kids and I collect fall leaves and use those too. I LOVE fall. Fall is the beginning of all the winter fun.

For spring and summer we celebrate by hanging our flags and decor, frequenting the local farms for all the wonderful produce that is available during these seasons.

We create little vacations with in our community. We are fortunate and have an Old Town Sacrament and river boats, big family farms and so much more. We can act like out of towners all the time.

Enjoy life, make it fun, it's short! Make great family memories.

Chapter 13

A Spiritual Practice is Free

Life is short, don't waste any of it. Find your happy place in the home and outside the home. Shop in places that make you feel good, go to parks that are clean, hang out with people that lift your spirits, practice daily gratitude.

In order to have a full, abundant life, one must have things right and in balance on the inside. Your mind has to be clean and filled with sunshine. Your heart must be singing the praises of life.

What I'm saying is that what your outside life looks like is a reflection of your inner world. You must, absolutely without fail, prioritize the healing or improvement of your mind. A healthy, happy, positive and grateful mind and a mouth that speaks words of encouragement and gratitude out loud will reap the benefits of a good life.

The Center for Spiritual Awareness has a little saying, change your mind, change your life. It all starts with our state of mind. That combined with our feelings and words. What do you focus on, what do you obsess over, what is it that you think about the majority of the day? This will be what is shaping your outside life. Your thoughts will make your life choices for you.

I have met a miserable cad or two and they would go on and on of their troubles and how life is just not good to them. True to their word, their life stank. They had the worst of luck, got fired, wife left, even the dog left. But don't feel too sympathetic. No, others have felt pity hearing these sad tales of woe, others would try and help. Funny thing is this...those sad saps usually didn't want the help; they don't even take any of the solution based advice. Turns out that they were very comfortable with their story and sad life. It worked for them.

Are you this sad lad or lady? Or are you the other person, that bright eyed gal with good things to say, are you of good cheer, that person that it seems like good things are happening for them all the time, good luck follows them around like an eager puppy.

Those happy people have a life to match. It's the Law of the Universe. It's in all religious and spiritual text, especially in the great Bible. A million, billion sayings and proverbs on what we think, what we speak is the life and world we will co create.

I truly believe that a spiritual practice of some sort is mandatory for inner peace and joy. You need faith in the hard times and blessings all the time. Spirit guides us, protects us, and provides for us in all ways and all the time. Tune in, connect.

God (or Spirit if that is more comfortable for you) is a beautiful thing. I love all the Avatars that have come here to teach us, Jesus, Buddha being two of the greatest. I love my spiritual life and I grow and heal and learn more every day. Since embracing a spiritual quest I have recreated my life completely. I was damaged goods and now I'm the cream of the crop.

Find a Church, a temple, a Center for Spiritual Living. Take classes, join a bible study, and meditate. There is so much out there. Make yourself your biggest project and all else will fall into place.

If you have issues with addiction, be it food or alcohol and a list of other things, get help. There is AA, NA, FA, OA...it goes on and on. It's free and can turn your life around. Not to mention that addictions can be very, very expensive! They are also the beginning of the end. The end of good credit, the end of marriages, the end of good parenting, good friendships, families and eventually the end of a life.

You can get help, counseling, support groups and all kinds of things for free. You just need to want to change and improve.

If you don't have anything heavy like addiction going on, but you are just not that happy, well get into a group, do volunteer work, order self-help books through the library, take classes through your Spiritual center. By the way, some Spiritual Centers and Churches teach classes on finances too.

A really healthy, clean diet is also big. If you eat crap you feel like crap and then you get fat and feel even more crappy. When we eat salads, clean foods and fruit and plenty of water through the day we feel light and cheerful. Really!

Get out and move! Dance, join a class. How about yoga at the community center? The community center offers all kinds of great classes for movement, dance and walking groups. You make new friends and the more you exercise the better you feel with all those endorphins, yay!

Make new friends. Some of the oldies are our golden treasures; tend to them like priceless jewels. My old friends know everything about me and that gives me comfort and stability. They have stuck it out through all weather. It's like a good and devoted marriage, in sickness and healthy, rich and poor. Then there are the friends you need to put some space between. Some pals just bring us down; downer Debbie's we call them. You don't need to throw them away, just limit the time. If you do have supper negative and mean friends, well, they aren't really friends. Drop em'.

New friends are fun too. As you grow and your interest change you will attract different people. Enjoy this new comradery. They can be supportive for new endeavors such as your new frugal life or a new sober life.

Work hard on yourself and you will become a better wife, husband, mother, father, worker bee, neighbor and so much more.

Use this book to the fullest to create a simple life free of the burden of debt, create a savings so that if hard times come you will be prepared. Whittle down all the business in your world down to the basics so you can really enjoy your life and your family and friends.

Change everything if it calls to you. Change jobs, change towns, change how you get to work, change groups that you hang out with. Find your happiness, thrive!

Hear no negativity, See no negativity, Speak no negativity.

One of the cheapest, easiest ways to change our lives without a group, therapy or a Spiritual Center is to just watch what we take in and what we put out into the world.

Everything you see, watch, listen to, speak of, think about, surround yourself with has an effect on your inner peace and even physical health. When we watch a movie we hold those images for years. What we think and speak creates a vibration. What we hold in can cause sickness and disease. It's a science really.

There are some videos you can watch if you are new to all this, even if you aren't new, a refresher is always good. I compiled a list of books and videos in the back of this book. There are websites where you can watch documentaries that teach about religion, spirituality, metaphysics and so on.

Don't poison yourself with toxic people, angry music and violent films. Don't do it!!!

Find friends and new people that are cheerful and grateful. Hang out with the blessed folk and do as they do. Listen to music that lifts you up and makes you want to dance and clean your house. Watch movies that are clean and sweet. Educate yourself on everything, especially the spiritual world.

Create a beautiful life! After all it doesn't cost a thing, but the rewards are worth millions.

Chapter 14

Paying off the Royal Debt

You would think that this would be the first chapter right? It's the last for 2 reasons; one being that I forgot about this crucial part until now and the second is that it turned out perfect this way.

You have assessed where all your money is going or was going, you've trimmed your bills, gotten rid of a few extras, trimmed the grocery budget, gone to an envelope system, cleaned out your home, maybe earned some cash on selling some furniture and such. You should be decluttered and organized at this point and ready for the next huge job. Tackling that debt! And now you should have some extra money to do it.

This will be a short chapter and the end for us folks, because I'm not a financial advisor and there are many ways to take care of debt. I used a nonprofit credit counseling company and, for me, that was great. I had letters, warnings, bills and calls coming faster than I could hide. What this company did was take care of all of my creditors (they have a legal team), got all my finance rates lowered, consolidated all the bills into one payment a month and it came out of my bank account automatically monthly. No more calls, no more mail, no more worry. I just had to make sure and have that money in the bank for the payment. I could choose how fast or slow I wanted to pay things off.

You will need to do your own research. Dave Ramsey seems to have some intelligent advice, so does Suzy Orman. There are others out there, but be careful, don't pay for anything. You can do free research and get free advice online and through the library and, like I said previously, some Spiritual Centers and Churches have classes on finances.

Some people consolidate all the cards on one card and then pay chunks on that one. Some pay off all the little cards until they just have the one big card. Some of us go to credit counselors. Be very careful and only go to the nonprofit and if they want large sums of money or a big percentage and use fear to motivate...hang up. Make sure you are going through a reputable company.

As soon as you pay off the debt you will feel such accomplishment and freedom. Get it done as fast as possible. Get the second job or do side jobs if you can hack it. This book will help you, the more you pinch pennies the more you will have to pay toward the debt.

I also strongly suggest you try to save at the same time. Always have a nest egg. Don't be the typical family that is one pay check away from poverty. Build up enough savings so that you could live off of it for months if something happened. This is another reason you want to cut all your expenses and housing cost. If you have a 5,000 dollar monthly mortgage, you can forget survival if you lose a job.

And of course there are tons of people on line that will share their stories of how they got out of debt. You have millions of friends out there just waiting to share their story and advice. Go get it!

Chapter 15

Tips and Secrets of the Wise

Here is a parting gift from me to you. It's all kinds of little tid bits of advice that I've learned from other more clever women and men or I've earned through experience in being a penny pinching Queen. Enjoy.

When towels get old either donate to an animal shelter or if you are super handy with the sewer, cut into smaller pieces and hem to make dish towels are many wash clothes.

When being extreme you can just ad coffee grounds to yesterday's brew to make another pot. You can get two or three brews off one filter.

Better yet, find a percolator at a thrift store or craigslist, Freecycle. These make great coffee and you never have to buy filters.

If you run out of filters, use a paper towel.

Use a top sheet for a bed ruffle. The sheet should be a size up from the mattress size. Example: a queen size over a full size box spring. Use a solid color so it goes with everything. (This is my auntie's tip).

Save plastic containers with squeeze tops for putting homemade sauces, salad dressings, mayonnaise you buy in bulk or anything you get in bulk. You put some in these containers to put on the table during meals.

Decorate for birthdays, holidays, baby showers, even weddings (believe it) from The Dollar and 99cent stores

Save all gift bags and tissue, wrap from parties. Start a gift tub. Save all cards sent from donations.

Reusing all plastic bags, grocery, bread, bulk, and produce...to reuse to line garbage, clean up dog doo on walks or in yard, to pack lunches, store things.

Putting a water filter on sink tap or getting a Britta pitcher for frig. Never buy bottled water. Carry your own bottle with ice or freeze night before.

Put dish detergent in another bottle with half water to make it last longer. It's concentrated so works great. You can do this with shampoo too.

Use cheap shampoo from The Dollar store as bubble bath.

In winter, after baking, leave oven open to give more heat to kitchen.

Hang up a clothes line outside to hang clothes in warm weather to save on electricity.

Use clothes pins to close open food bags.

Do trade for services or goods.

Start a coin jar and save all the loose change in the couch, wallet and pockets.

When splurging on a café coffee drink, choose coffee over a latte, you'll save a couple bucks.

Move close to work so you can walk or bike.

Plan your menu around all the sales at the store.

Use old socks for cleaning clothes.

Invest in a deep freezer. You can stock up on sale items and cook dishes ahead of time.

Buy a crock pot. Crock pots are great for simple home cooking. Throw all the ingredients in, turn on and then go about your day.

Get a bread maker. Make all your own bread, this can save a few bucks a loaf.

Buy frozen fruit and veggies. They are just as healthy as fresh and last much, much longer.

Add tons of vegetables to all your soups, casseroles, pasta dishes and meat or veg pies as a healthy filler. It can double a recipe and it gets your kids to eat more vegetables.

Use the envelope system for everything like gas, transportation, entertainment, vacations, holidays, even beauty such as haircuts, clothes and make up.

Grow your own flowers so you never have to buy a bouquet again.

Use YouTube and the library to learn how to fix or do anything inside or outside your home. Next time something breaks, don't call a repair man, see if you can do it yourself.

Learn a skill on the internet for free such as cooking.

Learn to crotchet or knit. You can make cheap gifts and clothes for your family.

Learn to sew. Mending and altering clothes saves pennies. Making clothes can be fun (I wouldn't know, but I've heard). You can even make the kids Halloween costumes.

Save the left over coffee in the pot. Store it in the frig for ice coffee later.

Make all your own cleaners and laundry detergent.

Use old newspaper for cleaning windows.

Bake up a whole chicken then divide into parts. You should be able to get a soup, a casserole or two and maybe enchiladas or burritos out of one chicken.

Mix half high quality dog and/or cat food with a cheaper brand to make it stretch.

Use old socks for cleaning rags.

Use candles at night when you've settled in for TV time, it's cozy and saves on electricity.

Invest in a steam mop of mop that has a Velcro cloth mop that can be thrown in the wash. You will never spend money on a mop again (unless the steam mop breaks).

Use dish washing rags that can be thrown in the wash instead of sponges. Sponges have to be replaced all the time and bread germs.

Buy an extra turkey after Thanksgiving when they are really cheap. Freeze and save for really tight times. You can make so many casseroles, turkey pies, turkey soups and so much more from one turkey. It can stretch the groceries a couple weeks.

Read The Complete Tightwad Gazette for hundreds more ideas.

References

Here are list of books that will help with financial over haul, domestic management and building a Spiritual inner life. I also have a list of movies that are incredibly inspiring.

Internet

Blissfulanddomestic.com (for domestic and budgeting advice)

daveramsey.com (for finances)

mrskatesingh.com (for everything)

Spiritual Videos and Resources

The Secret

What the Bleep Do We Know!? Down the Rabbit Hole

Secret of Water, Discover the Language of Life

GAIAMTV (for spiritual videos and documentaries)

Movies

The Pursuit of Happyness

Rocky

Peaceful Warrior

McFarlan, USA

Frozen (The Disney cartoon)

Groundhogs Day

Cinderella Man

Billy Elliot

The Blind Side

Dead Poets Societ

Books

The Complete Writings of Florence Scovel Shinn

Think and Grow Rich, Napoleon Hill

Success Through a Positive Mental Attitude, Napoleon Hill

The Law of Attraction, Esther and Jerry Hicks

Autobiography of a Yogi, Paramahansa Yogananda

The Bible

Awaken the Giant Within, Anthony Robbins

The Law of Success, Napoleon Hill

Skinny Bitch, Freedman and Barnouin (for the new vegan)

Hungry Girl Cookbooks (for the diet concious)

The Complete Tightwade Gazette, Amy Dacyczyn (my favorite for being frugal)

America's Cheapest Family, Steve and Annette Economides (also my favorite frugal book)

The Cheap Book, Robin Herbst and Julie Miller

The New Frugality, Chris Farrell

Cheap Talk with the Frugal Friends, Angie Zalewski and Deana Ricks

10,001 Ways To Live Large On A Small Budget, by the writers of Wise Bread

How to Decorate & Furnish Your Apartment on a Budget, Lourdes Dumke

The Small Budget Gardener, Maureen Gilmer

Printed in Great Britain
by Amazon

28316577R00053